Especially for

From

Date

Wit & Wisdom

for
Cat Lovers

Inspiration &
Encouragement
from
Our Feline Friends

Wit & Wisdom
for
Cat Lovers

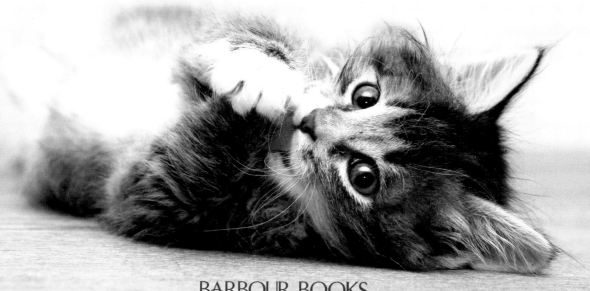

BARBOUR BOOKS
An Imprint of Barbour Publishing, Inc.

Awake and Waiting

My help comes from the LORD, who made heaven and earth. . . . He who keeps you will not slumber.

PSALM 121:2-3 ESV

Tigger has a daily routine to wake his mistress, Kim, every morning when he wakes up on the pillow next to her head. First, he crawls closer to Kim's body, stretches his whole paw out over her nose, and squeezes her nose gently, as if he were holding a Kleenex. Then if she still doesn't wake up, he projects one claw from the same paw and gently taps it on the bridge of her nose. He keeps tapping, gradually increasing in strength—as if he were an impatient person tapping his nails on a counter—until she wakes up acknowledging him with a good morning massage.

Erika's cat, Chena, knows morning wake up is the most difficult time for her mistress, too. So at first she gently pads around her head, back and forth on the pillow as if she were tracing and retracing a silhouette. If the slumbering giant remains motionless, she amps up her legs and moves faster and faster from side to side, adding a raspy purr for special effect. Erika awakens from her dreams as though she had been on a night sleeper in a roaring twenties railroad compartment as the engine shakes and sputters into a platform—its first stop of the day.

And she is alert enough to shake, rattle, and roll out of bed.

Recently Judith's new cat did something none of her cats ever had! She hit the bed from the floor with a super-cat hurdle and then plopped straight onto Judith's face—claws extended. Judith woke with a painful *ouch*! She reached up and touched her forehead, bleeding from the puncture wound. After cleaning off her first battle scar of the day, she surmised, "She must have forgotten to retract her claws. She has been pretty ruffled lately with the other cats."

Thankfully we don't have to devise some clever strategy each morning to wake up our Creator. We are assured He is going to care for our watering, feeding, safety, and general well-being. We can pray or cry for help at any time of the day or night, and we know He hears. Our Creator never slumbers or sleeps. He does not check out for a while to replenish Himself, like we—His critters—need to do regularly.

We need never worry about hurting our heavenly Father with words or a terrible entrance because of life's aggravations. He knows our situation better than we do. If we have had a recent fight with a prowling enemy or we are frantic to find safety, God is always awake and waiting to help us.

Good cat owners always introduce
their cats as members of the family.

FLUFFY

I have learned a lot from my cat. When life is
loud and scary, go under the bed and nap.
When you want someone to notice you, sit on
the book that person is reading. And if someone
sits in your chair, glare at her until she moves.

UNKNOWN

Any household with at least one feline
member has no need for an alarm clock.

LOUISE A. BELCHER

In peace I will lie
down and sleep, for
you alone, LORD,
make me dwell in safety.

PSALM 4:8 NIV

Even though I walk
through the darkest valley,
I will fear no evil,
for you are with me;
your rod and your staff,
they comfort me.

PSALM 23:4 NIV

Sin pays off with death.
But God's gift
is eternal life given by
Jesus Christ our Lord.

ROMANS 6:23 CEV

Blessings

And my God will meet all your needs according
to the riches of his glory in Christ Jesus.

PHILIPPIANS 4:19 NIV

All the cats are happy, but Frick is an example of a very contented
cat. Perhaps it is because of how he came to us that he seems to be
so thankful for our home. The window well is no longer his bed, and
he now receives regular veterinarian attention. Food is always plentiful,
and he doesn't have to depend on what he can catch or wonder when
he will eat his next meal. A warm house keeps him protected from the
elements. Instead of always being on guard, he sits with paws folded
under his body in deep contentment and trust of his circumstances.

Do we feel this much trust toward our heavenly Father? Are we
willing to allow Him to provide for our needs, accepting His provision
with gratitude and thankfulness? Sometimes, I am too independent in
my thinking, believing I have to do everything myself. By letting go a
little, and allowing God to bless me with His provision, I, too, can be
contented.

He gives food to those who fear him;
he always remembers his covenant.

PSALM 111:5 NLT

Unlike us, cats never outgrow
their delight in cat capacities,
nor do they settle finally for limitations.
Cats, I think, live out their lives
fulfilling their expectations.

IRVING TOWNSEND

Everything that moves serves
to interest and amuse a cat. He is
convinced that nature is busying
herself with his diversion;
he can conceive of no other
purpose in the universe.

F. A. PARADIS DE MONCRIF

For everything God created is
good, and nothing is to be rejected
if it is received with thanksgiving.

1 TIMOTHY 4:4 NIV

As for the rich in this world, charge
them not to be proud and arrogant and
contemptuous of others, nor to set their
hopes on uncertain riches, but on God,
Who richly and ceaselessly provides us
with everything for [our] enjoyment.

1 TIMOTHY 6:17 AMP

17

Claws In

Steve liked to refer to his multicolored long-haired cat as a brute, because that was the opposite of the cat's nature. The gentle pet had blue eyes and gray, brown, and white fur. Although she was a female, Steve named her Spike.

On the morning of Steve's wedding day, he was in his front yard with Spike at his feet. Two big dogs came running down the sidewalk toward them. Knowing this would freak out Spike, Steve bent over to pick her up and protect her. His touch, however, startled the nervous cat. Spike must have thought she was being attacked and responded in kind.

With claws at full alert, Spike ripped up her owner's hand with deep cuts, not scratches. Steve attended his wedding ceremony that evening with his right hand and wrist completely bandaged!

Because fear had distorted Spike's thinking, she had attacked her caregiver. I'm afraid I've done that with my Divine Caregiver. Despite His faithful love and provision, when life gets rough, my first instinct is to turn on Him.

Why won't You do something? I don't deserve this. How can You love me and let me suffer this way? It's not fair. I have even accused God of being mean. Looking back, if I had not misinterpreted Him, I would have known He was reaching out to hug me not hurt me.

Life is fearsome at times, but God is not a hard taskmaster who feeds us to the dogs. He knows what He's about. The difficulties He allows will produce a "harvest of righteousness and peace" (Hebrews 12:11 NIV) when I submit to His training process. Even when circumstances terrify me, I need to trust God's wisdom and keep my claws in.

The great charm of cats is their rampant egotism,
their devil-may-care attitude toward responsibility,
their disinclination to earn an honest dollar. In a continent
which screams neurotically about cooperation and the
Golden Rule, cats are disdainful of everything but their
own immediate interests and they contrive to be so suave
and delightful about it that they even receive
the apotheosis of a National Cat Week.

Robertson Davies

Sometimes all they want is some special sign of affection.
For instance, Pumpkin's dish may be full, you may have
scratched her behind the ears until your hand is ready to
fall off, but she keeps right on giving you a round,
insistent stare or meowing her fool head off.

Eric Swanson

Be still in the presence of the Lord, and
wait patiently for him to act. Don't worry about
evil people who prosper or fret about their
wicked schemes. Stop being angry!
Turn from your rage! Do not lose your temper—
it only leads to harm. For the wicked
will be destroyed, but those who trust
in the Lord will possess the land.
PSALM 37:7–9 NLT

Because you know that the testing of your
faith produces perseverance. Let perseverance
finish its work so that you may be mature
and complete, not lacking anything.
JAMES 1:3–4 NIV

Rightful Inheritance

You prepare a table before me in
the presence of my enemies.

PSALM 23:5 NIV

Arwen was a misfit cat in the Philippines. Even though he was an adopted stray into our American missionary home, he was not a Filipino cat—or at least he didn't see himself as one. Most cats in the Philippines have a status on par with the rodents they catch. Even though Arwen was just your average tabby alley cat, our Filipino friends would comment how nice his fur was and ask what breed he was (to our amusement!). To their surprise, we would then tell them that we fed him American cat food and that's the reason he looked so healthy.

Like most cats, Arwen enjoyed eating but was a picky eater. Sometimes Arwen would not eat all his food, leaving some in his dish for a later snack. He never, however, had the chance to finish his leftovers. Nightly, a giant bullfrog would squeeze its way under our screen door and help himself to Arwen's cat food in his dish. He would gobble up Arwen's food and then sit in the drinking water of the cat dish. This was one smart frog! Every time we shooed him away, he would return the next evening. It was like he was visiting his nightly bed and breakfast. Arwen had a pesky enemy.

Arwen, of course, did not like the fact that a giant frog finished off his food every night. But instead of chasing it away, he would just stare at it and then treat the frog with indifference. I thought that Arwen's cat instincts would surely kick in and he would give chase to this enemy, but he never did. So night after night, the bullfrog returned and feasted on Arwen's food. He let his enemy get the best of him.

God has also prepared a table before us in the presence of our enemies. But we need not look on them with indifference or be intimidated by them. We are His royal children and have every right to the blessings of the King of kings. Let's not allow our enemy to steal our blessings right from under our noses. Instead, let's claim our rightful inheritance and delight in the daily feast God has prepared for us. It is ours, free for the taking!

Cats must have comfy places to sit and
look out. To the dedicated bird-watcher,
nothing makes the time pass quicker,
and the whiskers twitch faster,
than the object of her natural, abiding
interest and careful study.

INGRID NEWKIRK

There's no need for a piece of
sculpture in a home that has a cat.

WESLEY BATES

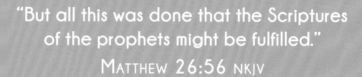

"But all this was done that the Scriptures
of the prophets might be fulfilled."

MATTHEW 26:56 NKJV

Everything God says is true—and it's a
shield for all who come to him for safety.

PROVERBS 30:5 CEV

A Gift

Do you not know that your bodies are temples of
the Holy Spirit, who is in you, whom you have received
from God? You are not your own; you were bought at
a price. Therefore honor God with your bodies.

1 CORINTHIANS 6:19–20 NIV

A cat's sense of smell is fourteen times more powerful than humans'. Most predators, including cats, track by smell. Feral cats, especially, will spend what seems to be an inordinate amount of time grooming themselves. What they are doing, however, is removing any evidence of food or other scent that may identify them to a potential predator. Grooming also rids the coat of dirt and parasites, such as fleas. And because cats don't have sweat glands, grooming aids in making them feel cooler on hot days.

Do we take care of our bodies as well as our cats? I know I don't. I sometimes take the gift of my body for granted, especially when it comes to eating healthy foods or getting enough exercise or rest. Next time I see Frick, Yoda, or Chewy grooming themselves, I will recommit to taking better care of the gift that God gave me—my body!

*Pay attention to
advice and accept correction,
so you can live sensibly.*

PROVERBS 19:20 CEV

Just as the would-be debutante will
fret and fuss over every detail till all is
perfect, so will the fastidious feline patiently
toil until every whisker tip is in place.

LYNN HOLLYN

It would be hard indeed to list all
the fascinating qualities attributed to
cats over the ages—especially since
every cat seems to have a unique
temperament. Nevertheless, most cats
share a few common characteristics. . .
dignity, complexity, empathy, grace,
presence, cleanliness, and charm.

ERIC SWANSON

Don't copy the behavior and customs of this world, but let God transform you into a new person by changing the way you think. Then you will learn to know God's will for you, which is good and pleasing and perfect.

ROMANS 12:2 NLT

"The LORD doesn't see things the way you see them. People judge by outward appearance, but the LORD looks at the heart."

1 SAMUEL 16:7 NLT

Furry Feet and a Purr

For he will command his angels concerning
you to guard you in all your ways.

PSALM 91:11 NIV

One Saturday evening, the two cats and I were in the living room, watching TV. George, my American shorthair, dozed on the sofa. Chloé, my petite Abyssinian, lay in my lap, cleaning her face with one paw. I was relaxing after a day of hard work unpacking boxes in our new home.

With no advance notice, both cats sat up and looked toward the other end of the house. They jumped down and took off down the hall in full hunt mode, running with bellies low to the floor. This was strange behavior for two house cats who never went outside, never hunted anything larger than a fly.

Quietly I followed them into the darkened bedroom to discover the reason for their actions. When I entered the room, I saw them both sitting on their haunches—side by side—looking at the windows in the wall facing the alley. Through the partially closed blinds, I could see a man walking down the alley, where he had no reason being.

I quickly dialed 911 and told the operator that someone was trying to break into my house. We exchanged the necessary information and she alerted the police to my emergency. To this day, I do not know what prompted her next question. She said, "Ma'am, are you scared?"

The truth was that I was scared, but not panicked. I knew that God was protecting me. My confidence in Him must have revealed itself in the way I was speaking. While all this was taking place, my faithful guard cats continued sitting between the man moving around in the alley and me. They followed the man's progress by moving their heads in unison, always facing exactly where he stood.

It may seem a little strange that my pets would act more like guard dogs than house cats. However, cats acting out of character to protect me are no stranger than crows feeding a prophet. We may not always see the angels God provides for our protection, but on that Saturday night, my angels had furry feet and a purr.

If you have a cat, congratulations. You have a relationship in which you are unconditionally loved, endlessly forgiven for your mistakes, never judged, and constantly entertained. A cat can make the stresses of your day disappear just by curling up in your lap at night.

Pam Johnson-Bennett

The reasons we share our lives with our cats may be different, and yet somehow they are tied by a common thread. It is love that links us together: love of the animals and their love for us, for reasons known only to them, but it's all the same. It's all love.

Sara Wilson

God stays one with everyone who openly
says that Jesus is the Son of God. That's how
we stay one with God and are sure that
God loves us. God is love. If we keep on
loving others, we will stay one in our hearts
with God, and he will stay one with us.

1 JOHN 4:15–16 CEV

This is real love—not that we loved
God, but that he loved us and sent his
Son as a sacrifice to take away our sins.

1 JOHN 4:10 NLT

Work Light

> Two are better than one, because
> they have a good return for their labor.
>
> ECCLESIASTES 4:9 NIV

I've learned that most people think that cats are natural hunters. The truth is that the ability to hunt for food is taught by the kittens' mother. Fortunately for Frick, Yoda, and Chewy, their mothers taught them well and they are all three excellent mousers.

Cats are usually solitary hunters, which was why I was so amazed at the several times I have seen all three of mine hunting collaboratively. One cat will circle around the back, while another keeps watch and the third is crouched and ready to move in. They work together like a well-oiled machine, reading one another's body language and instinctively knowing what to do next.

Just as the cats found, combining our energies and talents makes us both more efficient and likely to succeed. There is help in times when difficulties emerge and companionship during the good times. I know I have more fun when I work alongside others, and as the old adage says, "many hands make the work light."

Who is smart enough
to explain everything?
Wisdom makes you cheerful
and gives you a smile.

ECCLESIASTES 8:1 CEV

My soul mate was Captain. Together we caught frogs, climbed trees, hid from my brothers—we were a team. No one had ever told us the lie that cats are aloof, independent, or uncaring. Captain certainly never was. He comforted me when I was lonely; I cuddled him when he was. He was an incorruptibly fine soul, and I am the richer to have known him.

SARA WILSON

We can feel lonely with lots of others around. We may feel "not okay." It is easy to give up hope. We need to hear a voice that says, "I choose you." And the touch of a finger— or a paw—means so much.

MARTA FELBER

And He said to them, "Which of you shall have a friend, and go to him at midnight and say to him, 'Friend, lend me three loaves; for a friend of mine has come to me on his journey, and I have nothing to set before him'; and he will answer from within and say, 'Do not trouble me; the door is now shut, and my children are with me in bed; I cannot rise and give to you'? I say to you, though he will not rise and give to him because he is his friend, yet because of his persistence he will rise and give him as many as he needs."

Luke 11:5–8 NKJV

Building the Kingdom

Have confidence in your leaders and submit to their authority, because they keep watch over you as those who must give an account. Do this so that their work will be a joy, not a burden, for that would be of no benefit to you.

HEBREWS 13:17 NIV

Yoda likes to look out the window—and will sometimes sit there for hours at a time. Her eyes dart to and fro, looking at what may be in "her" yard. Sometimes her muscles will tense and I'll hear a low, guttural sound as she sees something that doesn't please her. While she could never defend us like a watchdog, her intent to defend her turf is no less sincere.

Matthew Henry says in his commentary on Hebrews 13:17 that we are to acknowledge that our spiritual leaders are not only there to teach and lead us in holiness, but to watch over everything that might be hurtful to our souls. They are to protect us by warning us of danger and Satan's tricks. This charge is of utmost importance. Loving, encouraging, and supporting our pastors and mentors in the building up of the kingdom is a responsibility we should all take seriously.

And a servant of the Lord
must not quarrel but be gentle
to all, able to teach, patient.

2 TIMOTHY 2:24 NKJV

A cat is a patient listener, even when you're
telling a story for the third time. A cat is the
most dependable alarm clock you'll ever have.
A cat will show you how to enjoy life. A cat
chooses the company he keeps.

PAM JOHNSON-BENNETT

In everyone's life, at some time, our inner fire
goes out. It is then burst into flame by an
encounter with another human being.
We should all be thankful for those
people who rekindle the inner spirit.

ALBERT SCHWEITZER

Jesus replied: " 'Love the Lord your God with all your heart and with all your soul and with all your mind.' This is the first and greatest commandment. And the second is like it: 'Love your neighbor as yourself.' All the Law and the Prophets hang on these two commandments."

MATTHEW 22:37–40 NIV

For everything comes from him and exists by his power and is intended for his glory. All glory to him forever! Amen.

ROMANS 11:36 NLT

A Restful Night

In peace I will lie down and sleep, for you
alone, LORD, make me dwell in safety.

PSALM 4:8 NIV

Chloé was a petite, mostly white Abyssinian. She had huge green eyes that seemed small under her oversized ears. The combination of large round eyes and jumbo ears gave her a waif-like look. Chloé never outgrew her playful ways. She always acted like a two-year-old—constantly chattering, eternally curious, and trying to be the center of attention any time guests came to the house. Her joyful zest for life kept laughter bubbling up in me as she batted her favorite paper ball around the house and under the furniture.

One night, I woke in the middle of the night to feel Chloé playing with something on top of the covers of my bed. I tried to get her to leave her toy and settle at my side, but she refused. *Oh well,* I thought, *she'll knock it off the bed in a minute and give it up.* It was wintertime and cold, so I didn't want to leave my nice warm bed to take her paper ball away from her.

As I lay there waiting for her to tire of playing by herself, I began to notice little sounds that were made when Chloé wasn't moving.

Curious to see what she was doing, I reached up and turned on the lamp. There in the middle of the bed was a palmetto roach. Chloé had heard this one in the kitchen, looking for a warmer spot, and had decided it would make a very nice toy to play with on my bed.

I took vigorous exception to her opinion. As soon as I saw this very-much-alive roach scurrying across the covers, I threw them back and scrambled out of bed. I quickly picked up a book to smash the bug, but we couldn't find it. Unwilling to get back in the bed without knowing the exact location of that roach, I pulled a blanket out of the closet and spent the rest of the night on the sofa.

Chloé stole my peaceful night's rest with her antics. Other distractions may be stealing your slumber, but the answer is always the same: Trust in the Lord for a night of rest. He can keep you safe, regardless of the type of thief that wants to steal your sleep.

If a man insisted always on being serious,
and never allowed himself a bit of fun
and relaxation, he would go mad or
become unstable without knowing it.

HERODOTUS

I think my favorite thing in the house
has to be the cat. . .mainly because
she's just like a big piece of noisy
Velcro when you toss her at the sofa.

MICHELLE ARGABRITE

"I am coming to you now, but I say these things while I am still in the world, so that they may have the full measure of my joy within them."

JOHN 17:13 NIV

Is anyone among you in trouble? Let them pray. Is anyone happy? Let them sing songs of praise.

JAMES 5:13 NIV

For our heart shall rejoice in Him, because we have trusted in His holy name.

PSALM 33:21 NKJV

A Better Friend

One who has unreliable friends soon
comes to ruin, but there is a friend
who sticks closer than a brother.

PROVERBS 18:24 NIV

After a serious accident and surgery, my husband was laid up for several weeks nursing his ankle. Accustomed to being very active, he didn't enjoy sitting around. Eventually, his inactivity would get the best of him, and he'd hobble around the house using a walker. Almost always, his foot would start to hurt and swell, and back to the couch he'd go to elevate his ankle on a pillow. Without fail, at least two of the cats would hop on the sofa, with one of them making a nest beside my husband, sometimes falling asleep beside him.

It seems our cats always know when we don't feel well. Their presence warms and comforts us as they minister to our souls with their soft fur and loud purrs. They do not judge us, but simply give of themselves to make us feel better.

Am I always an unselfish person to those I am friends with? I'm urged by my cats' example to be a better friend to my human companions.

Nevertheless God, who comforts the downcast, comforted us.

2 CORINTHIANS 7:6 NKJV

A dog will show his love by jumping on
you at the front door. A cat will show
his love by ignoring you, and then curling
up next to you when you need it most.

DANIELLE ASSON

A cat can be trusted to purr when
she is pleased, which is more than
can be said for human beings.

WILLIAM RALPH INGE

When I was in distress, I sought the Lord;
at night I stretched out untiring hands,
and I would not be comforted.

PSALM 77:2 NIV

Remember your promise to me; it is
my only hope. Your promise revives me;
it comforts me in all my troubles.

PSALM 119:49–50 NLT

Sit Firmly

Where there is strife, there is pride,
but wisdom is found in those who take advice.

PROVERBS 13:10 NIV

Spencer was definitely an alpha cat. He thought he was the alpha person in our household. He loved to lie in the flower boxes hanging off the balcony of our second-floor apartment to watch the world go by beneath him.

Several times a week, the owner of a large, male Doberman pinscher would walk his dog down the sidewalk in front of our apartment. This Doberman had a superiority complex, too. He was a fine-looking animal: large noble head and shiny black coat with tan markings. He pranced down the sidewalk and growled around his leather muzzle as soon as he and Spencer caught each other's eye. Spencer was too cool to reply. The only thing he moved was his tail as he flicked it back and forth out of the dog's sight.

This state of affairs changed dramatically one Saturday morning. My husband was setting the table for breakfast when he looked up to see Spencer disappear over the end of the flower box. Immediately from below came the sounds of yelping and growling and cursing so mixed up together that it was hard to tell which was the dog and which the person.

My husband dropped the silverware and ran down the stairs. In front of the building was an irate man holding back his angry dog. Spencer crouched on the ground not far away, shaking his head to clear the blood from his nose. As my husband scooped up Spencer, the dog's owner proceeded to tell him in tones and words quite unkind, that we should keep our cat away from his dog because the dog might not be wearing a muzzle the next time.

My daughter, Julie, heard the rest of the story later that day. Spencer had jumped down on the back of the Doberman, sank his claws into him, and was biting the back of the dog's neck. The dog's owner, while trying to control the frantic dog, hit Spencer on the nose to make him let go of the dog, jerked him free of the dog by Spencer's collar, and then threw him out of the dog's reach.

Spencer let his pride get him into a quarrel he could only lose. God protected him when the Doberman should have chewed him up. The next time our pride gets in the way of peace, we can remember Spencer and the alpha fight and then sit firmly on our pride.

Cats have a curious effect on people. They seem
to excite more extreme sentiments than any other animals.
There are people who cannot remain in the room with a cat—
who feel instinctively the presence of a cat even though
they do not actually see it. On the other hand, there are
people who, whatever they may be doing, will at once get
up and fondle a cat immediately [when] they see it.

ARTHUR PONSONBY

Do you see that kitten chasing so prettily her own
tail? If you could look with her eyes, you might see her
surrounded with hundreds of figures performing complex
dramas, with tragic and comic issues, long conversations,
many characters, many ups and downs of fate.

RALPH WALDO EMERSON

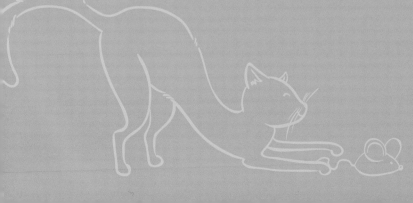

Finally, brethren, farewell. Become
complete. Be of good comfort,
be of one mind, live in peace; and the God
of love and peace will be with you.

2 CORINTHIANS 13:11 NKJV

If you are tired from carrying
heavy burdens, come to me
and I will give you rest.

MATTHEW 11:28 CEV

Forever Home

"My Father's house has many rooms; if that were
not so, would I have told you that I am going there
to prepare a place for you? And if I go and prepare
a place for you, I will come back and take you to be
with me that you also may be where I am."

JOHN 14:2-3 NIV

All of our cats were born in the wilds of our backyard and had feral parents. The idea of coming inside to live was an odd idea to them at first. It was a maze of rooms that contained frightening things. The television and vacuum cleaner were two foreign objects that caused our cats to go into hiding. Eventually, they got used to everything, and Frick even watches television now. Where we live is now their home, a place they associate with being fed and cared for. They know that their "forever home" means love.

Jesus talked about our "forever home" and described it as a real place where we would live with Him someday. He has lovingly prepared it for our arrival, and we will feel nothing but the love our heavenly Father has for us.

"God blesses those who mourn,
for they will be comforted."

MATTHEW 5:4 NLT

Although all cat games have their rules and rituals,
these vary with the individual player. The cat,
of course, never breaks a rule. If it does not follow
precedent, that simply means it has created a
new rule and it is up to you to learn it quickly
if you want the game to continue.

SIDNEY DENHAM

Cats nurture, watch over, and play with us as if
we were babes who didn't know how to take care
of ourselves—and certainly didn't have a clue
about when to indulge in a rollicking good time.

ALLEN AND LINDA ANDERSON

Though you have made me see troubles,
many and bitter, you will restore my life again;
from the depths of the earth you will again bring me up.
You will increase my honor and comfort me once more.

PSALM 71:20–21 NIV

Teach them to do everything I have
told you. I will be with you always,
even until the end of the world.

MATTHEW 28:20 CEV

Truth in Love

All you need to say is a simple "Yes" or "No."
JAMES 5:12 NIV

"In our neighborhood, cats are not allowed to roam free." I listened to Elizabeth recall the day she and Max, her handsome declawed blue point Siamese, paraded down the street in his royal blue harness, to call on his favorite feline.

Elizabeth knocked on the door. Max's taupe body tensed and his black nose twitched. Jayne, Miss Kitty's master, welcomed them inside. The visitors scanned the house from the entry hall and waited.

"Where's Miss Kitty?" No sooner had Elizabeth asked the question than a long-haired, black-and-white feline sauntered out, head held high. She walked past Elizabeth, turned slowly, and stopped a few feet from Max. Max's ears tilted back as he stepped quietly forward and faced Miss Kitty. He gazed into her creamy distant eyes for a moment and slowly pressed his lips on hers.

Jayne and Elizabeth winked at each other, entranced. They had never seen Max kiss Miss Kitty. For a moment, the beautiful girl stood motionless before her suitor. Then, without a sound, she turned away, trotted past Elizabeth, and disappeared into the next room.

Moments later, Miss Kitty reappeared. Again she pranced by Elizabeth, assuming her position in front of Max. Elizabeth loosened the lead on Max's leash. Again the suitor pressed his lips on Miss Kitty's cherub mouth—and pulled away for his final gaze.

Miss Kitty picked up one paw and swatted Max swiftly on the cheek. He jerked back in surprise. Frowning, she turned and padded off. Max, his eyes wide in disbelief, looked up to Elizabeth, dismayed. But Elizabeth and Jayne couldn't sympathize—they stood crying with laughter. Haven't we all experienced Max's dismay at misunderstanding from poor communication between families, friends, peers at our workplace, or social circles?

How many of us have had interpersonal relationships where we have been absolutely floored? We missed the feedback or misinterpreted the information from someone close to us. We said or behaved in a manner that was once acceptable and even encouraged by someone we connected with, only to discover what worked in the autumn disgruntles in winter?

When we look to God, dumbfounded by misunderstandings, He stands ready through His Holy Spirit to comfort, guide, and grant us insight as we pray. God knows our hearts. He can reveal when best to approach a person we have offended and how to speak truth in love.

When you've been working too hard, a cat will
walk across your papers to let you know it's time
for a break. A cat will show his gratitude for the simplest
act, such as scratching him under the chin, by serenading
you with his deep, rich purr. A cat will still adore you
on those days when you look your worst.

PAM JOHNSON-BENNETT

Few things bring out the passion in people
like cats. Many humans adore felines as they
adore no other creature. There is an intimacy
to cats—a club only they can invite you to join.
It is the feeling that I am a trusted and special
friend, fully sanctioned to enter a private world.

SARA WILSON

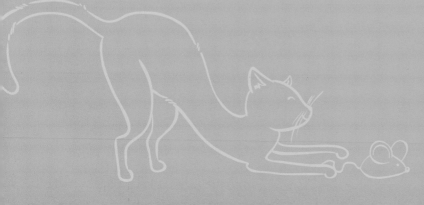

Show me a sign for good, that those who hate me may see it and be ashamed, because You, Lord, have helped me and comforted me.

PSALM 86:17 NKJV

I find true comfort, Lord, because your laws have stood the test of time.

PSALM 119:52 CEV

Praise be to the God and Father of our Lord Jesus Christ, the Father of compassion and the God of all comfort, who comforts us in all our troubles, so that we can comfort those in any trouble with the comfort we ourselves receive from God. For just as we share abundantly in the sufferings of Christ, so also our comfort abounds through Christ.

2 CORINTHIANS 1:3–5 NIV

Listen!

"Stand at the crossroads and look; ask for the ancient paths, ask where the good way is, and walk in it, and you will find rest for your souls. But you said, 'We will not walk in it.' "

JEREMIAH 6:16 NIV

Talia loves eating green grass. With the advent of spring rains and sprinklers, the lawns around my apartment turn positively lush. Even though she's an inside cat, Talia knows when springtime has come.

On a typical morning, I have to open the door pretty wide to exit with everything I have to carry. And as soon as Talia hears the locks tumble, she darts between my feet and out the door. I have no ability to chase after a fast-acting cat, due to arthritis. . .nor do I have time, because I only open the door when I'm leaving home. What should I tell my boss? "The cat made me late" isn't a valid excuse.

I go back inside, shutting the door behind me. Because, like cats everywhere, Talia hates closed doors—especially when it's the door that leads to her food dish. Usually that brings her running. But when she's feasting on grass, even the closed-door trick doesn't work.

Talia, of course, doesn't understand why I don't want her outside. Cats make tasty tidbits for the coyotes and foxes that roam our suburban neighborhood. She might also get outside and never make it home again. After all, she was a stray when she was brought to the animal shelter.

All Talia understands is that I'm angry with her when she goes outside—something she considers a natural and even desirable destination. Just as I know going outside is dangerous for Talia, God warns me about behaviors that could bring me harm. Also like my cat, I tend to ignore those warnings because I think I know better. The next time God warns me about something, maybe I should listen.

At times, cats seem like hairy little people.
In times of sickness or sorrow they may wrap your
head in their paws, nuzzle your neck, or lick your cheek.
A calm atmosphere is deeply linked to survival. If you are
upset or ill, your cat will do whatever it takes to soothe
you, so that his home becomes secure once more.

ERIC SWANSON

The purr is at the heart of our close relationship
with the cat. However, there are few early historical
references to purring. One does occur in the eulogy
to Beland the cat, written by Joachim du Bellay in the
mid-sixteenth century: "He was my favorite plaything/And
not forever purring/A long and timeless/Grumbling litany."

ROGER TABOR

Christ encourages you, and his love comforts you. God's Spirit unites you, and you are concerned for others.

PHILIPPIANS 2:1 CEV

You will increase my honor and comfort me once more.

PSALM 71:21 NIV

God is not a God of disorder but of peace.

1 CORINTHIANS 14:33 NIV

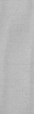

Be Wise

The wise fear the LORD and shun evil,
but a fool is hotheaded and yet feels secure.

PROVERBS 14:16 NIV

Spencer was an American shorthair cat who thought he was a full-mane African lion. Even the way he moved—that rolling shoulder walk, eyes searching ahead—looked leonine. He had that self-confident attitude that, for lack of a better word, I call presence. He lived up to his advertising, too. He assumed his rightful place in our household without being a bully and was friendly without being a nuisance.

Spencer was an indoor cat. We lived in a second-floor apartment with a balcony that had flower boxes built into the railing. When the weather was nice, we would allow Spencer out on the balcony. He would promptly leap into the flower box and lie there in the sunshine, watching the world go by below him.

One particular spring day, Spencer had watched several fat, lazy pigeons eating crumbs on the lawn that fronted the building. The birds were aware of Spencer and were careful to keep what they thought was a safe distance from our balcony when they took off and landed. Finally, one pigeon got careless and came close enough for Spencer to take a flying leap out of the flower box and catch it in midflight, with nothing under the feline but fifteen feet of air.

I learned about this when my daughter, Julie, went screaming out of the apartment, flying down the stairs, to see if her cat was alive. When I looked over the balcony railing, I saw Julie on the ground beside a stunned, but conscious Spencer and a dead bird.

Julie carried Spencer, seemingly unaffected by his experience, back upstairs. He did not get to keep the bird, which I am sure disappointed him. It was a long time before he was allowed back out on the balcony.

Many times, I act like Spencer, recklessly depending on my own abilities to get me through a foolish activity. All the time, God wants me to seek Him and avoid evil. That is the very definition of a wise person. May God grant us enough common sense to learn to be wise.

A cat is a very special friend who comes into
your life. When it comes it brings warmth, companionship,
contentment, and love. Whether it's long-haired,
short-haired, pedigreed, or "Heinz" makes no difference.
A cat, though independent, has a way of letting you
know that without you, life just wouldn't be worthwhile.

SHARON LUNDBLAD

May there always be a cat to comfort you when
you are sad, to amuse you when you are bored, to keep
you company when you are lonely, to remind you that a nap
in the sun is a fine thing, and to show you that the natural
world is always just a purr and a pounce away.

BRIAN KILCOMMONS AND SARA WILSON

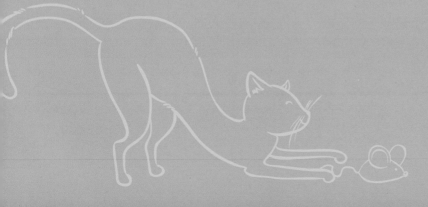

Give thanks to the LORD, for he is
good! His faithful love endures forever.
Cry out, "Save us, O God of our salvation!
Gather and rescue us from among the nations,
so we can thank your holy name and rejoice
and praise you." Praise the LORD, the God
of Israel, who lives from everlasting to
everlasting! And all the people shouted
"Amen!" and praised the LORD.

1 CHRONICLES 16:34–36 NLT

Worship the LORD with gladness.
Come before him, singing with joy.

PSALM 100:2 NLT

95

Bask in the Stillness

He says, "Be still, and know that I
am God; I will be exalted among the
nations, I will be exalted in the earth."

PSALM 46:10 NIV

"Have you seen the cats?" is a question I hear often. I check several places, including our three bedrooms. A favorite hangout is the top of a short bookcase, right next to a sunny window in the office. Sometimes the cats sleep there, but most often, this is their quiet place. Warmed by the sun with a view of the yard, the cats have learned to just "be" in this place. To be still, relax—maybe even reflecting on all that is going on in their world.

I am not very good at being quiet. I am always busy. Too busy, oftentimes, to take in the beauty that is God's creation. My cats teach me to take time to be quiet and to bask in being still—to stop my hands from work and fully feel the presence of God and His Word for me. And. . .perhaps. . .to sit by that sunny window for a few minutes.

Who would believe
such pleasure from
a wee ball o' fur?

IRISH SAYING

Cats are way above begging for food.
Cats prefer the direct approach when it comes
to getting our fair share—by being yowling, insufferable
pests, or just hopping up and helping ourselves.

JOE GARDEN

Cats speak a subtle language in which few
sounds carry many meanings, depending on how
they are sung or purred. "Mnrhnh" means comfortable
soft chairs. It also means fish. It means genial
companionship. . .and the absence of dogs.

VAL SCHAFFNER

If you are cheerful, you feel good;
if you are sad, you hurt all over.

PROVERBS 17:22 CEV

All the days of the desponding and
afflicted are made evil [by anxious thoughts
and forebodings], but he who has a
glad heart has a continual feast
[regardless of circumstances].

PROVERBS 15:15 AMP

Our LORD, let your worshipers rejoice
and be glad. They love you
for saving them, so let them always
say, "The LORD is wonderful!"

PSALM 40:16 CEV

101

Enjoy the Water Holes

The LORD is good to all; he has
compassion on all he has made.

PSALM 145:9 NIV

Everybody has a favorite room in the house. Tigger the tabby's room happens to be the bathroom. It didn't take Kim long to discover her rescue cat had an affection for water. When Kim bathed in the tub, Tigger eagerly perched on the edge, staring intently into the water as if it were a great fishing hole. That is, until he realized the personal benefits bathtub water could provide. Kim winced at the horrible screeches Tigger sometimes made while she was bathing—until one day she discovered what drove him to make the awful sounds.

She dipped her hand into the bathwater and cupped it until she wet his head. He continued the meow howl. Then she decided to try and scoop up more water. This time she wet his head, neck, and back, giving him a sponge bath fit for Puss 'n Boots. He stopped his call of the wild and purred contentedly.

She discovered the secret code to transform her disgruntled screecher into a prancing, contented cat. And although the toilet water doesn't contain the natural homeopathic cures of the bathtub basin, it does provide a source of study for the adventurous side of Tigger.

Kim noted that Tigger always liked to stare, mesmerized, at the rapidly circulating water in her porcelain cylinder after a good flush, as if it were a river whirlpool ready to pop up something from the rich depths of the hole.

One day as Kim stood washing her hands at the sink, Tigger stood beside her on his back legs, with his right paw on the toilet rim and his left paw on the lever of the toilet. He pushed down forcefully with his left paw, trying to emulate Kim's swift, successful flush—only moments earlier. Nothing happened. His strength was not that of his master. Only once, months later, did Kim again catch Tigger in the same place, same position, and with the same unsuccessful results on the toilet handle.

How many times do we fritter away our energy, attempting to do something that we were not created to do? God can make a water hole—but we'll never figure it out. Maybe we can enjoy our corner of the world as much as Tigger if we know when to sit back and enjoy the water holes and when to stop striving, keeping our paws off the levers of life that only our Master can operate.

Most pets display so many humanlike traits and emotions it's easy to forget they're not gifted with the English language and then get snubbed when we talk to them and they don't say anything back.

STEPHENIE GEIST

My cat exhibits all kinds of behavior normally associated with dogs. He fetches and retrieves sticks, understands and reacts to commands, chases people and dogs down the street, and eats all sorts of things that cats shouldn't like. Do I have a cat? Or is he a dog in disguise?

CAROL SMITH

105

So the ransomed of the LORD shall
return, and come to Zion with singing,
with everlasting joy on their heads.
They shall obtain joy and gladness;
sorrow and sighing shall flee away.

ISAIAH 51:11 NKJV

Long ago your own people did these
same things to the prophets. So when this
happens to you, be happy and jump for joy!
You will have a great reward in heaven.

LUKE 6:23 CEV

Evil people are trapped by sin,
but the righteous escape, shouting for joy.

PROVERBS 29:6 NLT

107

A Desire Check

He has given us his very great and precious
promises, so that. . .you may. . .[escape] the
corruption in the world caused by evil desires.

2 Peter 1:4 NIV

Spencer was the stereotype of a lion. He may have looked like a
house cat, but he didn't act like one. Spencer believed that being
domesticated was okay, if it didn't get in the way of what he wanted
to do, which was escape the apartment. He was too proud to crowd
around our feet and dart out of the door. He was too smart to think
that would be a successful method of escape. Nevertheless, he did
escape; and the first time he got out, I thought one of the girls had
failed to close the door properly.

"Julie," I yelled over the balcony, "look for Spencer! The door was
left open and he got out."

Julie and her friends quickly searched the stairwell, recovered the
cat, and returned him to the apartment. Julie also firmly denied leaving
the door open.

One afternoon not too long after Spencer had started escaping,
I heard some scratching noises on the landing outside the door. I
opened it to see Spencer playing with a mouse between the doors

of the two apartments. When I opened the door, Spencer became distracted just long enough for the mouse to escape and to squeeze under my neighbor's door.

I scooped up Spencer and knocked on the door. As soon as it opened, I said, "I'm sorry, but a mouse ran into your apartment." Stepping in and looking around, I spotted the mouse under the dining room table. While wrestling the twisting, yowling, angry ball of fur in my arms, I quickly got between the dining room table and the door to the kitchen. My neighbor ran for her broom, and her two children started jumping up and down and squealing. It was just too much for the poor little mouse. He dashed out the door and down the stairs.

As you can imagine, our neighbors were angry at Spencer's mouse-catching efforts. We promised to keep a closer eye on him. However, he continued to get out of the house, and we didn't know how he did it. Eventually, we discovered that Spencer was opening the door himself by jumping off a nearby bookshelf and holding down the door handle. From then on, we always kept the door locked.

Spencer's desire to escape the apartment led him into risky situations, but he was determined to have his own way. The next time you want to escape from your circumstances, do a quick check of your desires. If they are selfish ones, you may find that, just like Spencer, getting what you want causes you even more problems than you had before.

What a treat it is to see cats lie upside down
and bump their rumps from side to side. I think
it means they have just won the lottery. I always
check in the cat bed for a winning stub.

INGRID NEWKIRK

Apparently, through scientific research, it has been
determined that a cat's affection gland is stimulated
by snoring, thus explaining my cat's uncontrollable
urge to rub against my face at 2 a.m.

TERRI L. HANEY

So now we can rejoice in our wonderful
new relationship with God because our Lord
Jesus Christ has made us friends of God.

ROMANS 5:11 NLT

The LORD is my strength and my shield; my heart
trusted in Him, and I am helped; therefore my heart
greatly rejoices, and with my song I will praise Him.

PSALM 28:7 NKJV

"Until now you have not asked for anything
in my name. Ask and you will receive,
and your joy will be complete."

JOHN 16:24 NIV

Songs of Deliverance

You are my hiding place; you will protect me from
trouble and surround me with songs of deliverance.

PSALM 32:7 NIV

We moved. For weeks, we cleaned out cabinets and drawers. We packed boxes and bags. We evaluated our furnishings, much of which had been scavenged from the streets around our Brooklyn apartment. Several pieces went back out onto the street.

T-Tat was curious, snooping into piles and boxes and finding new places to snooze. My wife charmed the grocery store owner around the corner, and we made several trips to our new place, rolling our boxes down the street in a couple of borrowed carts. The last weekend, a friend loaned us his SUV, and we transported the few pieces of furniture we were keeping. On the final trip over, we took T-Tat and her things.

Transition is hard for everyone. T-Tat cautiously picked her way around cartons, located her food and water bowls in the new kitchen, and tried out the windowsill that looked out over the new backyard. A couple of mornings after the move, I couldn't find the cat. Bathroom? No. Under the sofa? No. In any windowsill? No. Waiting outside the closed bedroom door, just in case we had changed the no-cats-in-the-bedroom rule in the new place? Again, no. I feared we had left a door open, but both were shut and locked. Where was the cat?

Finally, I resorted to the classic fallback maneuver of cat owners everywhere. I went into the kitchen and jiggled her food bowl, as though I was putting out fresh food. She appeared immediately, which did not surprise me. But I was quite startled by where she appeared from. She had plunged to the floor from above me. Where had she been? Napping on the fridge?

Later, unpacking and finding places for our belongings, I again missed T-Tat. I went back to the kitchen and checked the top of the refrigerator. Nope. But, with a closer look, I did notice, way up in the eight-inch space between the ceiling and the cabinet tops, a couple of furry gray cat ears.

"T-Tat?" I called softly. No response. I jiggled her bowl. Down she flew. It seemed unfair to trick her that way again, so she got a couple of cat treats. Poor girl. All the parts of her life had changed. Everything looked different and smelled different and was different. So, she went looking for a safe place to retreat, away from the disarray and disorganization, where things were quiet, and sometimes, if you waited long enough, people put food in your bowl.

Lives are full of things that make us search for a haven of rest. A shift in jobs or relationships or financial status can make us feel insecure. But God is with us through constancy and change. When we feel overwhelmed, we do have a Hiding Place, and Someone who will surround us with songs of deliverance, which can be just as satisfying as a handful of kitty treats.

Happiness is like a cat. If you try to coax
it or call it, it will avoid you. It will never come.
But if you pay no attention to it and go
about your business, you'll find it rubbing up
against your legs and jumping into your lap.

WILLIAM BENNETT

When you're special to a cat, you're special
indeed. . .she brings to you the gift of her
preference of you, the sight of you,
the sound of your voice, the touch of your hand.

LEONORE FLEISHER

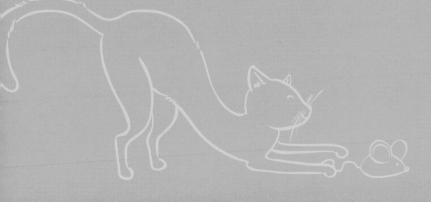

Singing psalms and hymns and spiritual songs among yourselves, and making music to the Lord in your hearts.

EPHESIANS 5:19 NLT

May God give you more and more grace and peace as you grow in your knowledge of God and Jesus our Lord. By his divine power, God has given us everything we need for living a godly life. We have received all of this by coming to know him, the one who called us to himself by means of his marvelous glory and excellence.

2 PETER 1:2-3 NLT

Balance

A cheerful heart is good medicine,
but a crushed spirit dries up the bones.

PROVERBS 17:22 NIV

The rattle of a ball as it rolls across the floor is followed by the *thumpty-thump* of an orange cat chasing after it. Frick then hops up on the coffee table and is mesmerized by how a writing pen twirls when he swats at it with his paw then follows it as it drops to the floor. He discovers that the pen doesn't twirl the same way as it did on the table. Chewy starts to chase his sister, Yoda, their sleek, black forms leaning into the curve as they round into the hallway. Both slide on the hardwood floors, which makes the chase that much more fun.

Our cats love to play! Just like their human counterparts, play is enjoyable and oftentimes involves imagination. It also helps to release pent-up energy and is good exercise. But, more than that, it makes us happy!

Our Father God knows we need to have times of play, to relax, smile, and be lighthearted. Having fun helps us balance life with work and other difficult activities, and brings us joy. Now, where's that ball?

The sacrifice that honors me is a thankful heart. Obey me, and I, your God, will show my power to save.

PSALM 50:23 CEV

Seize the moment of excited curiosity on
any subject to solve your doubts; for if you
let it pass, the desire may never return,
and you may remain in ignorance.

WILLIAM WIRT

A kitten is so flexible that she is almost
double; the hind parts are equivalent
to another kitten with which the forepart
plays. She does not discover that her tail
belongs to her until you tread on it.

HENRY DAVID THOREAU

Therefore, as God's chosen people, holy and
dearly loved, clothe yourselves with compassion,
kindness, humility, gentleness and patience.
Bear with each other and forgive one another
if any of you has a grievance against someone.
Forgive as the Lord forgave you. And over all these
virtues put on love, which binds them all together
in perfect unity. Let the peace of Christ rule in
your hearts, since as members of one body you
were called to peace. And be thankful.

COLOSSIANS 3:12–15 NIV

Don't use foul or abusive language.
Let everything you say be good and
helpful, so that your words will be an
encouragement to those who hear them.

EPHESIANS 4:29 NLT

Only God

Trust GOD from the bottom of your heart; don't try
to figure out everything on your own. Listen for GOD's
voice in everything you do, everywhere you go;
he's the one who will keep you on track.

PROVERBS 3:5–6 MSG

Puddin' was a petite, multicolored cat with a sweet disposition and a happy-go-lucky attitude that made her special, if only to us. She wasn't a beautiful cat; in fact she wasn't exceptional in any particular way; that is, until she had kittens.

Puddin' really took to motherhood. Unlike some cats, she seemed to sense this was a higher calling. She was determined to protect and provide for this little brood, no matter how difficult the task. The kittens were born in a comfy box, which we placed inside a large wooden storage building with windows. After the last kitten was born, we left the new mom and babies resting quietly, certain that we had provided safe accommodations.

Apparently Puddin' didn't agree. When we returned to feed her, we found the box empty. After a desperate search, we found she had moved to another box, one filled with stuffed animals. A quick head count showed that several kittens were missing. Muffled cries told us they were on the bottom of the box, covered with a mountain of toys. We carefully took them out and placed each one back in the original box.

At the next feeding, we found she had once more moved the kittens, this time to a dangerously high shelf. We brought them down, placed them on a blanket in the middle of the floor near several clean boxes, and left. We hoped she might choose one of the boxes and put the kittens in without our meddling. But by the next day, we watched in horror as Puddin' climbed down the side of the building, a full twelve feet high, with a screaming kitten in her mouth. She was apparently on her way to find another "safe" spot for her family.

Unless we heed the advice in Proverbs, we could spend much of our life like Puddin'—rushing down the wrong path, hoping to arrive at the right place. God knows that even our best tries, apart from His leading, will turn out badly. But if we listen to His voice and allow Him to direct our steps, we will remain on track. That's just the kind of comfort and assurance that we all need and only God can provide!

I have noticed that what cats most
appreciate in a human being is not the ability
to produce food, which they take for granted—
but his or her entertainment value.

GEOFFREY HOUSEHOLD

I woke up this morning to the sound of two
cats entwined in a roly-poly play fight making
their snowball way down the hall until they
separated only to chase each other back around
and start all over again. And I have to admit,
I wished I could be a part of the gymnastics.

CAROL SMITH

If you remain in me and my words remain in you, ask whatever you wish, and it will be done for you. This is to my Father's glory, that you bear much fruit, showing yourselves to be my disciples.

JOHN 15:7–8 NIV

Not unto us, O LORD, not unto us, but to Your name give glory, because of Your mercy, because of Your truth.

PSALM 115:1 NKJV

Unconditionally

Whoever does not love does not
know God, because God is love.

1 JOHN 4:8 NIV

Our cat named Frick lived in the window well when we bought our home, so he "came" with the purchase. It took over a year of soft conversation, food, and careful touching before he'd consent to come into the house. About a year after Frick's conversion, another of our feral-turned-house cats gave birth to the litter that included Yoda and Chewbacca. These cats had the benefit of knowing human companions early on, so their entry into our home was much less difficult.

However, that first winter with all of them in the house consisted of a lot of back arching, hissing, and scratching. Things have settled down substantially since our furry children came to live with us, but the whole situation made me consider what God asks of us—to put aside differences to love one another unconditionally. When we value another over ourselves, we please our Father.

I love cats because I love my home and after a while they become its visible soul.

JEAN COCTEAU

Cats, with their shining eyes and silent footfalls,
have always eluded explanation. Throughout
the several thousand years of shared history between
cats and human beings, cats have been a source of
wonder and unease, reverence and superstition.

STEPHEN BUDIANSKY

The dog is a pack animal. He hunts in a pack
and his whole social structure is built on the
pack mentality. A cat, on the other hand,
is a sociable animal but not the pack
animal that a dog is. His social structure
is built upon his sense of territory.

PAM JOHNSON-BENNETT

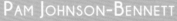

Tell everyone of every nation, "Praise the
glorious power of the LORD. He is wonderful!
Praise him and bring an offering into his temple.
Worship the LORD, majestic and holy."

1 CHRONICLES 16:28–29 CEV

And now, dear children, continue in him,
so that when he appears we may be confident
and unashamed before him at his coming.

1 JOHN 2:28 NIV

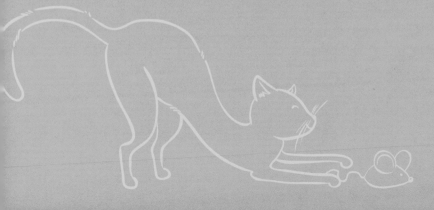

Ever Faithful

His compassions never fail. They are new
every morning; great is your faithfulness.

LAMENTATIONS 3:22–23 NIV

In Hawaii, Cindy's varicolored cat named Kate loved to go to the beach. She would swat at the waves when they washed up to where she stood and pat the bubbles left behind. She liked to dig in the sand with both front paws, looking for hermit crabs.

Another thing about Hawaii that Kate loved were the geckos that clung to walls inside the house. But Kate had the unfortunate habit of biting their tails off. A gecko's tail grows back, but guests in Cindy's home would see a tailless gecko and ask what happened.

"We have a cat," Cindy would tell them. That explained it.

Although Kate tormented geckos, she had a gentle, affectionate nature. When she rubbed against someone's leg, Cindy called it a "cat-hug." Whenever someone reached down to pet her soft fur, Kate would roll on her back like a dog to have her tummy stroked.

These favorite things made Kate unique. When Cindy moved to Utah, however, Kate no longer had the beach or geckos to play with. No more ocean waves to swat back or crabs to find. And no more tails to taste. Everything had changed. Except her owner's love. Kate still had Cindy taking care of all her needs, holding and petting her, talking to her, and scratching her head.

Sometimes life throws major changes our way. We lose things we love and have to go on living without them. Many times an unexpected event forces us to give up places or people we enjoyed. Our losses may be permanent, but so is God's love.

The older we get, the more changes we have to adjust to, but one thing will never change—the steadfast love of God. The hymn "Be Still My Soul" states: "In every change He faithful will remain." I don't think Kate misses gecko tails so much. Not when she has Cindy to stroke her belly every day.

Everything that is new or uncommon raises
a pleasure in the imagination, because it fills
the soul with an agreeable surprise, gratifies
its curiosity, and gives it an idea of which
it was not before possessed.

JOSEPH ADDISON

We tie bright ribbons around their necks,
and occasionally little tinkling bells,
and we affect to think that they are as sweet
and vapid as the coy name "kitty" by which
we call them would imply. It is a curious
illusion. For, purring beside our fireplaces
and pattering along our back fences,
we have got a wild beast as uncowed and
uncorrupted as any under heaven.

ALAN DEVOE

We suffer in the hope that you will be comforted and saved.
And because we are comforted, you will also be comforted,
as you patiently endure suffering like ours. You never
disappoint us. You suffered as much as we did,
and we know that you will be comforted as we were.

2 CORINTHIANS 1:6–7 CEV

For you know that we dealt with each of you
as a father deals with his own children, encouraging,
comforting and urging you to live lives worthy of
God, who calls you into his kingdom and glory.

1 THESSALONIANS 2:11–12 NIV

Unlovelies

And when the Pharisees saw it, they said
unto his disciples, Why eateth your Master
with publicans and sinners?

MATTHEW 9:11 KJV

When our first three children were small we noticed that they were quite drawn to the cats on the farm, and we began to discuss the possibility of bringing a kitten to the house as a pet. So when our nice mama cat weaned a batch of kittens, my husband selected one and brought her home. The kids were thrilled and promptly named her Mingo.

Personally I have always liked cats, but with three young kids and plans for more, I couldn't see the wisdom in making this an indoor cat. Plus part of the purpose of the kitten was to keep the mice at bay. However, she was not completely tame at this point, and we were afraid she would return to her family before the kids had the opportunity to love her into submission. That is why my husband decided to use a large animal cage for a short while. We made sure the kids understood that Mingo was to be in the cage when they weren't playing with her. We warned them that she might run off if they weren't careful.

They took our admonition seriously. Very seriously. One afternoon, shortly after Mingo's arrival, I was doing some housework. The baby was asleep, and my son was spending time on the tractor with Daddy. I noticed that my daughter Moriah was being very quiet. That is always cause for alarm as she is not known for being quiet—even while she sleeps. I began my investigation and soon discovered her whereabouts. She had locked herself inside the cage with her new little buddy, and they were spending quality time together.

Many different things ran through my mind at that moment. Even while laughing, I was wondering how Moriah had managed such a feat. Being our little Houdini I'm sure she would have just as easily made her escape when she was ready. I also remember very distinctly thinking how gross it was that my beautiful two-year-old child was inside a cage with a cat.

She had no qualms about it herself. For a small child she had a very large vocabulary, and she let me know in no uncertain terms that she wanted to play with Mingo, but she didn't want Mingo to run away, so she thought it would be best to spend the afternoon in the cat's cage. What was I to do besides laugh and grab the camera?

Unfortunately as Christians, we're not always quite so understanding. We're quick to pass judgment on those who would reach out to the "unlovelies" of this world. All too often we take on the form of "Christian" snobbery, and we expect other Christians to do the same. In that, we're no better than the Pharisees.

We should be careful to get out of an experience only the wisdom that is in it—and stop there; lest we be like the cat that sits down on a hot stove lid. She will never sit down on a hot stove lid again—and that is well; but she will also never sit down on a cold one.

MARK TWAIN

The popularizing of the cat by writers and artists such as Edward Lear and Beatrix Potter has made them endearing images for children's pets. Edward Lear was so devoted to his cat Foss that when he moved, his new villa was constructed exactly like his old house so as not to inconvenience his cat in any way!

ROGER TABOR

For I am convinced that neither death nor life,
neither angels nor demons, neither the present nor the
future, nor any powers, neither height nor depth,
nor anything else in all creation, will be able to separate us
from the love of God that is in Christ Jesus our Lord.

ROMANS 8:38–40 NIV

"I will praise you, LORD. Although you were
angry with me, your anger has turned
away and you have comforted me."

ISAIAH 12:1 NIV

"I will turn their mourning into gladness; I will
give them comfort and joy instead of sorrow."

JEREMIAH 31:13 NIV

Tell Somebody!

Give thanks to the LORD and proclaim his greatness.
Let the whole world know what he has done.

1 CHRONICLES 16:8 NLT

Living on two acres of wooded property, we were accustomed to animal sounds. But one day, after listening for only a few seconds, we realized what we were hearing didn't fall into the "normal" category. It sounded more like the screams of something small and without hope.

A quick survey of the front yard revealed a beautiful gray kitten with long hair, stubby legs, and small pointed ears. He looked more like a baby owl than anything in the feline family. We went toward him, expecting him to run, but instead he just sat there. We bundled him in a towel, for his warmth and our safety, and took him to a nearby vet.

An examination revealed that this very young kitten was dehydrated, nearly starved, and apparently close to death. His wailing had been a last-minute cry for help. The doctor hooked him to various tubes, but warned us that he couldn't guarantee anything. We left wondering if he would make it through the night.

The next day we were told that the kitten was eating and seemed stronger. Realizing this had probably taken several of his nine lives, we decided to bring him home and nurse him back to health. Thus began our relationship with this large-eyed kitten that looked like something that had fallen to earth from a nest in the trees. We called him Hooty.

At first, Hooty wasn't sure he could trust us. He would scurry from spot to spot, hiding under furniture to watch our activities from a safe distance. But after a few weeks of care, and probably a hundred bowls of kitten food, he began to respond with love. . .lots of love. He was totally devoted. His actions implied that he realized, somehow fully understood, that he would have perished had someone not heard his cry.

God heard our cry. Through Jesus, He has shown us how deeply He loves us and His plan for our salvation. It's more than we can comprehend, and it's something we never deserved. Our gratitude and thankfulness should overflow, making it impossible for us to remain quiet. God has provided hope and healing for a hurting world—let's tell somebody!

The cat does not offer services. The cat
offers itself. Of course he wants care and shelter.
You don't buy love for nothing.
Like all pure creatures, cats are practical.

WILLIAM S. BURROUGHS

Friendship is unnecessary, like philosophy,
like art, like the universe itself (for God
did not need to create). It has no survival
value; rather it is one of those things
which give value to survival.

C. S. LEWIS

Cats have intercepted my footsteps at
the ankle for so long that my gait, both at
home and on tour, has been compared to
that of a man wading through low surf.

ROY BLOUNT JR.

As iron sharpens iron, so one
person sharpens another.
PROVERBS 27:17 NIV

Two people are better off than one, for they
can help each other succeed. If one person falls,
the other can reach out and help. But someone
who falls alone is in real trouble. Likewise,
two people lying close together can keep each
other warm. But how can one be warm alone?
ECCLESIASTES 4:9–11 NLT

And my God shall supply all your need
according to His riches in glory by Christ Jesus.
PHILIPPIANS 4:19 NKJV

Rescued

So, as those who have been chosen of God,
holy and beloved, put on a heart of compassion,
kindness, humility, gentleness and patience.

COLOSSIANS 3:12 NASB

Clearwater, Florida—hot and muggy, with a threat of thunderstorms—was an unfriendly place for a solid black, stray cat lurking on the beach behind the restaurant next to our condo. The poor creature was desperate for food and fresh water. My son, David, knew as soon as he spotted the feline in need, he must rescue this pitiful ball of fur.

David rushed to the condo to find a can of tuna and bowls for food and water. Then he returned to the beach, praying to find the cat still there. He was so thankful when he spied him digging around a trash bin, searching desperately for food. In David's mind he had already named him Buster. Patience and compassion were needed to coax Buster to trust him. Eventually David got close enough to catch the cat—but not without much feline clawing, hissing, and fighting. As they entered the condo, Buster rushed to the window and climbed the drapes. The only recourse was to lock him in the bathroom while David prepared a bed and safe place for him.

But Buster would not be tamed without loads of loving kindness. When anyone came to the door, there were howls of protest. Upon receiving guests, he climbed David's leg, leaving claw marks before reaching his shorts. His exploits included hiding in a storage bin on the balcony for days before we could locate him, ravished and thirsty; and hiding under the bed, unwilling to come out even with the enticement of delicious treats.

Buster's first trip to the veterinarian is legendary in that office. Now when it's time for Buster to visit the vet, he is given what amounts to valium for cats. The vet and his assistant don protective gloves that cover to the elbow. Then—and only then—are they ready to examine Buster.

You might wonder if this cat was worth rescuing. He has been a reluctant captive at best. David bears the marks of Buster's defiant ways. There is no accounting for the boy's love of the cat. With determination, however, David captured Buster's heart. Now there is a mutual love and respect between the cat and the boy. Buster has come to realize he has been rescued.

God's love for us sinful, defiant creatures, is infinite. He pursues us for a love relationship. He rescues us from the pit of hell for a future with Him, now and for eternity. Just like Buster, we are thankful to be rescued.

Before a cat will condescend
To treat you as a trusted friend,
Some little token of esteem
Is needed, like a dish of cream.

T. S. Eliot

I rarely meddled in the cat's personal
affairs and she rarely meddled in mine.
Neither of us was foolish enough to
attribute human emotions to our pets.

Kinky Friedman

159

Ask, and it will be given to you;
seek, and you will find;
knock, and it will be opened to you.

Matthew 7:7 NKJV

Examine me, O Lord, and prove me; test my
heart and my mind. For Your loving-kindness is before
my eyes, and I have walked in Your truth [faithfully].

Psalm 26:2–3 AMP

More Marvelous

See what great love the Father has lavished
on us, that we should be called children
of God! And that is what we are!

1 JOHN 3:1 NIV

While my children and I sat in church one Sunday morning, our cat sat outside on the window ledge and wailed louder than the choir. I commissioned my ten-year-old son to capture her and take her across the yard to our mobile home on the church property. It wasn't till after church that we realized the reason for the concert. Frisky (don't blame me, my daughter named her) had had her kittens and apparently forgotten where she put them. Each time she crawled into a box, bag, or behind the couch, we thought, *Eureka!*, but nothing.

That night, when I tucked my two children into bed, they asked about the baby kittens. Would they be okay? As a busy mom I've been absentminded at times, but I never forgot where I put my children. "Mama Cat will find where she put her kittens," I reassured them, hoping I was right. We'd been having warm spring days, but it was still a bit nippy at night.

At last, I sat down in the kitchen with a hot cup of tea, glad to have a quiet moment. And then I heard them. So much for the quiet moment. In my pj's and slippers, like a cat burglar, I tiptoed outside around our trailer with a flashlight and promptly dismantled part of the skirting. Shivering, I hunkered down and peeked underneath, with images of spiders and snakes dancing in my head. "Come out, come out, wherever you are." I was answered by some desperate mewing above my head.

I'm sure Frisky meant well when she hid her kitties between the floorboards and insulation. I fetched a knife from the kitchen, hoping that my neighbors wouldn't be watching and worrying from their windows. I crawled back into the trailer's underbelly and carefully cut through the black plastic. I pulled out two adorable kittens crying for all they were worth, one tiger striped, the other, looking very Halloween-ish, black with orange dots.

I marveled at how I felt about those two noisy bits of fluff, both of which could easily fit inside my teacup. I felt as if I'd acted as midwife and delivered those kittens myself. But even more marvelous is how much God loves us frail humans. I left the comforts of home and crawled under a trailer in the cold blackness and stuck my hand up into the unknown. How much more intense and passionate is His love for us, for Jesus to leave heaven and come to earth to deliver us!

When we honestly ask ourselves
which person in our lives means the
most to us, we often find that it is those
who, instead of giving advice, solutions,
or cures, have chosen rather to share
our pain and touch our wounds with
a warm and tender hand.

HENRI NOUWEN

Cats grace us with their affection. . . .
When they curl up on your lap, it's because
they think you're worth spending time with.
When they climb onto your shoulder,
it's because they trust that you will carry them
safely. When they lie across your magazine,
it's because they can't believe their best friend
would rather look at this flat, boring thing
than their sleek, gorgeous, purring selves.

BRIAN KILCOMMONS AND SARA WILSON

We have confidence in the Lord that you
are doing and will continue to do the things
we command. May the Lord direct your hearts
into God's love and Christ's perseverance.

2 Thessalonians 3:4–5 NIV

"For the Lord your God is living among you.
He is a mighty savior. He will take delight in you
with gladness. With his love, he will calm all your
fears. He will rejoice over you with joyful songs."

Zephaniah 3:17 NLT

167

Precious

"The LORD your God is with you, the Mighty Warrior
who saves. He will take great delight in you;
in his love he will no longer rebuke you,
but will rejoice over you with singing."

ZEPHANIAH 3:17 NIV

When I was in high school, I practiced my clarinet every day. I was
good—really, I was. I even made first clarinet in the all-state band. . .so
don't assume anything based on my cat Mike's behavior. Whenever
I sat down and began to blow, Mike jumped on my lap. He rubbed
against my fingers, making it impossible for me to play. When I did
manage to extricate my digits from his rubbing, he "sang" right along
with my clarinet. But if I wanted to get any serious practice time in,
Mike had to go outside.

Fortunately, Talia, the cat who currently claims me as her human, feels
differently about my music. (The fact I'm not playing a clarinet might
help.) I'm the prototypical songbird in the shower. Get me under hot
water, and music flows out of me. When I'm bored, I sing. "Ninety-nine
splashes of water to go, ninety-nine splashes to go. . . ." I generally make
it out of the bath with about "forty" to spare, and continue singing to
see if I can finish dressing before I run out of splashes.

Talia's favorite time to spend with me is when I'm getting dressed. She casually approaches the door to my room and lies down so that only her seal-point ears or tail can be seen. I woo her into the room. "Twenty-five splashes of water to go. . .Talia, Talia, twenty-four splashes to go." At the sound of her name, Talia's ears bend forward. By the time I've repeated it two or three times, she has abandoned her carefree posture and joined me at my feet, meowing at every mention of her name.

Other times I croon in a singsong voice, "Talia, she is a girl. Talia, she is a pearl. Talia, she has no curls." When she meows, I agree, "I know, cats don't have curls." Sometimes we continue playing the game throughout the day, when I'm sitting at the computer or unpacking a box. When she hears her name, she takes it as an invitation to join me wherever I am.

I sing to Talia because she is precious to me and because I love it when she knows I'm talking to her. Zephaniah says God feels the same way about us. God quiets us with His love; He rejoices over us with singing. Like a father singing a lullaby to his baby. Or like me singing to my cat.

To anyone who has ever been owned by a cat,
it will come as no surprise that there are all
sorts of things about your cat you will never,
as long as you live, forget. Not the least
of these is your first sight of him or her.

CLEVELAND AMORY

Even the shiest cat craves her owner's affection.
While you're busy typing away or engrossed in
a video, she may just crawl out from her hiding
place under the bed and touch her nose to your
bare foot or rub her whiskers against your
shin—just to make sure you're there.

ERIC SWANSON

171

"I will heal their waywardness and love them freely,
for my anger has turned away from them."

HOSEA 14:4 NIV

That is what the Scriptures mean when they say,
"No eye has seen, no ear has heard, and no mind has
imagined what God has prepared for those who love him."

1 CORINTHIANS 2:9 NLT

And hope does not put us to shame, because
God's love has been poured out into our hearts
through the Holy Spirit, who has been given to us.

ROMANS 5:5 NIV

As a Child

"You will nurse and be carried on her arm
and dandled on her knees. As a mother
comforts her child, so will I comfort you."

Isaiah 66:12–13 NIV

My son's family cat, Pinkie, is a study in contradictions, starting with his name. Whoever heard of naming a black tomcat with a tiny white stripe under chin and belly Pinkie? When I asked his owner, my granddaughter Shannon, she said, "We didn't know he was a boy when we named him." I wouldn't have named a mainly black cat of either gender "Pinkie," but perhaps the image of a tiny tongue flicking around his bewhiskered face inspired Shannon's childish thinking.

In spite of his tough tomcat exterior, Pinkie's a big softie inside. He always befriends me, an occasional guest in his house. One day Shannon told me, "You can have Pinkie, if you like." I explained the facts of life to Shannon. My Talia prefers her solitary existence. Besides, I'd have to pay a big deposit for a second pet.

In spite of my objections, Pinkie must have approved of Shannon's idea. When I prepared to leave, I found him waiting on the roof of my car. (If he wanted warmth from the engine, wouldn't he have chosen the hood?) He blinked his yellow eyes at me as if to say, "I'm ready to leave." The next time I visited, he climbed back on the roof as if determined to make his home with me.

Even though I didn't adopt Pinkie, he still allows me to be his friend. When the house is quiet and the baby asleep, Pinkie indulges in one of his favorite pastimes. He climbs onto my lap and settles in for a nice long cuddle. He starts out in my lap, but soon creeps up my chest, places his front paws on my shoulders, and begins licking my ear and kneading my skin.

My son theorizes that Pinkie was weaned too young. When he finds an accommodating human, he pretends he's a baby again. Instead of being a grown tom, he imagines he's a helpless kitten enjoying the comfort of his mother's protection.

Like Pinkie, at times we wish we could curl up in our mothers' laps and let them comfort us. As adults, we have long since outgrown that recourse. But regardless of our age, we can always go to God as a child seeks out her parent; and He will take us in His arms and comfort us.

If having a soul means being able to feel
love and loyalty and gratitude, then animals are
better off than a lot of humans.

JAMES HERRIOT

If the pull of the outside world is strong,
there is also a pull toward the human. The cat
may disappear on its own errands, but sooner or
later, it returns once again for a little while,
to greet us with its own type of love.

LLOYD ALEXANDER

The birth of a kitten is one of the most
moving events you can see. New life
offers an opportunity to enjoy innocence,
trust, and love generously given.

MORDECAI SIEGAL

177

Finally, brethren, whatever things are true, whatever things are noble, whatever things are just, whatever things are pure, whatever things are lovely, whatever things are of good report, if there is any virtue and if there is anything praiseworthy—meditate on these things.

PHILIPPIANS 4:8 NKJV

For we are God's masterpiece. He has created us anew in Christ Jesus, so we can do the good things he planned for us long ago.

EPHESIANS 2:10 NLT

The LORD will guide you always; he will satisfy your needs in a sun-scorched land and will strengthen your frame. You will be like a well-watered garden, like a spring whose waters never fail.

ISAIAH 58:11 NIV

179

True Sanctuary

He is my loving God and my fortress,
my stronghold and my deliverer,
my shield, in whom I take refuge.

PSALM 144:2 NIV

Marie had a gorgeous long-haired albino cat with a flat pink nose. Daily her puffball tore rapidly up and down the hallway at the speed-of-white—earning the name Snowball Express. Each sprint ended with a precision dive under Marie's queen bed, braking suddenly, strategically positioned. Safe from the reach of human intruders, he squatted perfectly centered under the mattress. Snowball Express seemed to purr with pride after his exercise routine. He hunkered down happy for the day, always a step ahead of his owners—or so it seemed.

Unknown to her cat, one day Marie's mom lent the bed to the pastor of their church. He carted it off in the evening. The following morning at the appointed time, Snowball Express raced down the hallway to his favorite sanctuary. He made a dive, then assumed camouflage position—only to discover his cover was gone.

He slowly looked to the left, then to the right as he realized his whole body was exposed. Not only was the mattress gone, but the frame. Probably feeling the ventilation, he inched his head up and gazed at Marie—standing above him, grinning. His face contorted in horror, his kitty jaw dropped, and his eyes grew as big as saucers. He squatted under—nothing—only empty space all around him and the ceiling of the room useless at ten feet above his head.

What do we try to hide behind that is only a temporary refuge? We place our trust in our jobs for provision—jobs that can end as the seasons turn. We depend on our farms to provide crops for food, while the farmer looks to the weather report for success.

Invest in heaven, store your treasures above where they cannot be lost or stolen, Jesus taught us. We can all get stuck in a rut of routine and forget, as we race through our days, that everything we have on earth is temporary. How much more valuable to build up eternal rewards that can never be taken away and find true sanctuary in our Creator.

Cats are the ultimate narcissists. You can tell this by all the time they spend on personal grooming. Dogs aren't like this. A dog's idea of personal grooming is to roll in a dead fish.

JAMES GORMAN

The cat has been described as the most perfect animal, the acme of muscular perfection and the supreme example in the animal kingdom of the coordination of mind and muscle.

ROSEANNE AMBROSE BROWN

So God created man in His own image,
in the image and likeness of God He created
him; male and female He created them.

GENESIS 1:27 AMP

You, LORD, are our Father.
We are nothing but clay, but you
are the potter who molded us.

ISAIAH 64:8 CEV

Let love be your highest goal!
But you should also desire the
special abilities the Spirit gives.

1 CORINTHIANS 14:1 NLT

Every Minute

"Behold, I stand at the door and knock; if anyone
hears My voice and opens the door, I will come in
to him and will dine with him, and he with Me."

REVELATION 3:20 NASB

I shared an apartment with my tuxedo cat, Sammy. Aside from not
kicking in his share of the rent, he had all the best attributes of a
roommate anyone could want. He didn't borrow my clothes, leave dirty
dishes in the sink, or take long showers depleting the source of hot
water. He was a faithful fellow, too. I knew when I let him out in the
evening, I could trust him to come home before midnight—most of the
time.

We had a system worked out. As I lay in bed reading, he
announced he was ready to come in, hopefully without a fresh-caught
"gift." Not by sitting by the back door and meowing, mind you. Oh no,
not dramatic enough for this active kitty. Sammy chose the bedroom
window, which had no windowsill for him to hop on to, and body-
slammed himself with a loud *THA-FONG!*—his silhouette splayed on
the window behind the curtain as he clung to the screen.

The back door of the apartment was at the foot of my bed. At
his signal, I would crawl over to the foot and open the door. In thirty

seconds, he unclenched his claws, dropped to the ground, and trotted inside.

One night, Sammy was later than usual. I was about to open my door to call him, when the familiar *THA-FONG!* pounded not far away. No silhouette appeared on my window. The man in the next apartment yelled, "Wha-? What's that?"

I opened my door. "Sammy!" I whispered. "Over here!"

He unclenched his claws from my neighbor's screen and dropped to the ground, scampering to me. I closed my door as the neighbor opened his. Unaware, or unconcerned, that he had disturbed the neighbor's sleep, Sammy stretched, washed his face, and hopped up on the bed. He yawned and blinked up at me as I stood breathlessly by the back door. He seemed to say, Aren't you coming to bed?

The next day, my neighbor knocked on my door. "Did you hear that noise last night?" he asked.

"Yeah." I offered no explanation and hoped Sammy's aim would improve in the nights to follow. Forget about keeping him in at night. Some battles aren't worth fighting.

I don't know why Sammy went to the wrong window that night. But it's comforting to know that Christ is never at the wrong door. He knows exactly where we are every minute of the day and is ready for us to invite Him in to share His bounty.

The cat is surprisingly similar to
other high-tech devices you may
already own. Like personal digital
assistants, it is compact and portable.
Like a home security system, it is capable
of functioning autonomously for extended
periods without direct human intervention.
But unlike virtually any other product. . .
it is, for the most part, self-cleaning.

DAVID BRUNNER AND SAM STALL

It is easy to understand why
the rabble dislike cats. A cat is
beautiful; it suggests ideas of luxury,
cleanliness, voluptuous pleasures.

CHARLES BAUDELAIRE

Be honest in your judgment and do not decide at
a glance (superficially and by appearances);
but judge fairly and righteously.

JOHN 7:24 AMP

Your beauty should not come from outward
adornment, such as elaborate hairstyles and
the wearing of gold jewelry or fine clothes. Rather,
it should be that of your inner self, the unfading
beauty of a gentle and quiet spirit, which is of
great worth in God's sight. For this is the way the
holy women of the past who put their hope in
God used to adorn themselves.

1 PETER 3:3–5 NIV